South Plains Quilters Guild

In July of 1976, Betty Arper coordinated an all-day quilting bee as a Special Event at the Mahon Library. Area quiltmakers brought quilts for display and demonstrated methods of quiltmaking. The event aroused so much interest that several of those present decided to organize a quilting group.

An advertisement was placed in the newspaper inviting interested quiltmakers to attend and bring quilts, both old and new. The meeting was held in the Garden and Arts Center on January 25, 1977. Approximately 40 persons attended and displayed about 100 quilts, and gave the history of each quilt.

An organizational meeting was set and on March 1, 1977, the group was formed. The Quilting B's was chosen for the name. Betty Arper was elected president.

On October 8, 1978, the name of the organization was changed to The South Plains Quilters Guild. Dot Lawson served as the first president of the new guild.

Marilyn Ernest, Dot Lawson, Sue McGann, Sharon Newman, Jane Quade, Jackie Reis, and Betty Royal are charter members who are still active in the guild.

Lubbock, Texas, is located in West Texas at the southern end of the Texas Panhandle. Agricultural, medical, and educational opportunities draw people to Lubbock from a broad area surrounding the city, including eastern New Mexico. The Museum, Texas Tech University and Ranching Heritage Center showcase the history of the area. The guild participates in community activities including the annual Lubbock Arts Festival, Ranch Day and Candlelight at Christmas. Annual exhibits of quilts are hung in the Mahon Library with occasional exhibits in the Garden and Arts Center. Quilts made by guild members hang in the local Ronald McDonald House.

The SPQG Logo was designed by Carrie Lou Holtman. The banner was constructed by Martha Spears, Edna Thompson, Donna Locke, Syble Tarrance, and Carrie Lou Holtman. The Windmill block signifies the importance of water to the semi-arid region around Lubbock. The border is quilted with cotton bolls—cotton being the major money crop of the area.

General Directions

In this fast-paced world where everyone wants to get everything done quickly and easily, hand piecing can be an enjoyable and relaxing way to make a quilt. You can sit in your favorite chair, put your feet up, turn the television on and start sewing. Hand piecing can also be done anywhere. Carry your fabric pieces, needle and thread wherever your go and before you know it, you will have finished a block, two blocks, and then, a whole quilt.

Note: *Since the quilts in this book have been pieced by hand, the patterns for templates do NOT include seam allowance.*

Hand Piecing

Making Templates

To make templates for hand piecing, trace each pattern needed carefully onto see-through template plastic. Cut out along drawn lines, **Fig 1**; this will be your stitching line. **Note:** *Templates for hand stitching are cut WITHOUT seam allowances.*

Fig 1

Cutting Fabric

Place templates (without seam allowances) at least ¹/₂" apart on wrong side of fabric, **Fig 2**. Trace with a fabric pen or pencil, a #2 pencil or a .05mm mechanical pencil. Use a white or silver pencil for dark fabrics. Cut out shapes ¹/₄" from the drawn line to allow for seam allowance.

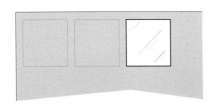

Fig 2

Threading the Needle

Cut an 18" length of a good quality cotton or cotton-covered thread at an angle and thread this end through the needle. Use a fairly short needle (#9 and #10 are the most popular).

To make a small, consistent knot for piecing and quilting, place the end of the thread cut from the spool (to prevent using the thread against the way it was wound) between your fingertips against the needle, **Fig 3**. Wrap the thread tightly two or three times around the needle, **Fig 4**. Pinch the wraps and pull the needle up through the wraps, **Fig 5**. A small knot will form at the end of the thread. Trim any excess thread beyond the knot.

Fig 3

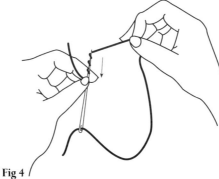

Fig 4

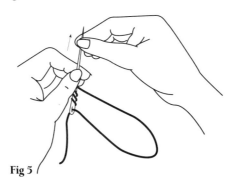

Fig 5

Piecing the Patches

When hand stitching two pieces together, begin by matching the drawn sewing lines of each piece, placing them right sides together; pin through the line on the top piece, matching the line on the bottom piece, **Fig 6**. Place pins at each end of the stitching line and enough times in between to avoid slippage, **Fig 7**.

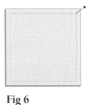

Fig 6   **Fig 7**

Stitch only on the marked lines using simple running stitches, **Fig 8**. Try to make eight to ten stitches per inch, but the most important thing is to keep your stitches as even as possible. Knot thread or make two or three backstitches, **Fig 9**, at each end. If a seam is very long, it is a good idea to made a few backstitches at various places along the seam as you sew. Press the seam allowance to one side, usually toward the darker fabric.

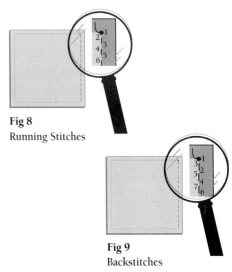

Fig 8
Running Stitches

Fig 9
Backstitches

When you approach a seam allowance, take a small backstitch and bring the needle up at the very end of the seam. Put needle through seam allowance to the end of the seam line on the next shape, **Fig 10**; backstitch and continue sewing. The seam allowance remains free to press in either direction.

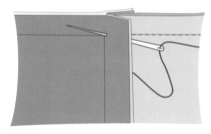
Fig 10

How to Add Borders (not ruffles)

Borders that lay flat with smooth corners are easy to achieve with some measuring.

1. After the blocks have been set, fold the bottom of the quilt up to the top to see if they are the same measure. Fold the quilt in half lengthwise and see if the sides are the same length. Minor differences can be accommodated, but if you have big differences, check why and correct seams in joining the blocks or adding the setting strips.

2. Measure the width of the quilt on the center fold. Measure in inches the length of the quilt on the lengthwise center fold. Cut the borders to this measure, allowing for seams, and two inches for insurance. (It is easy to cut this off later, but a nuisance to piece on another ³/₄" if there is a problem!)

3. Mark the center of each edge of the quilt with a pin. Starting with sides, fold the top portion of the quilt top toward the center and place a pin at the quarter measure; repeat for lower portion of quilt. Again fold top toward center and mark eighths; repeat for lower portion. Mark top and bottom edges of quilt top in same manner, **Fig 11**.

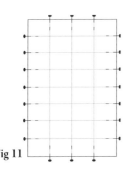
Fig 11

4. Mark the center of each border piece. Then, using the measurement (in inches) of the eighth marks on quilt top, mark the border strips, leaving one "insurance" inch at each end, **Fig 12**.

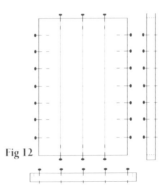
Fig 12

5. Pin the side border to the quilt at the center, quarters, eighths, and then as many pins as you need in order to stitch without stretching the border. If you had a slight difference in the border measurements, "ease" in the extra fabric equally over the length of the border. Stitch border to sides of quilt. If you are not mitering the corners, repeat for the top and bottom borders.

How to Miter a Corner

Mitered corners are especially nice when you are using a striped fabric for framing blocks or for borders.

1. Cut border strips the length and width of the quilt plus twice the width of the border strips, adding a couple inches in length for insurance. For example, if the length of your quilt is 60" and your borders are 2" wide, cut side border strips 60" plus 4" (twice the border width) plus 2" (insurance) for a total of 66".

2. Center border so extra fabric is at each end.

3. Sew border strips to sides of quilt beginning and ending ¹/₄" from each edge of quilt top, **Fig 13**; backstitch at each end. Press.

Fig 13

4. Fold the quilt diagonally right sides together matching the edges of the fabric in the border. Pin to keep the border edges together. Use a 45 degree angle to mark a line from the intersection (of the two seams attaching the border) to the edge of the border.

5. Pin along the mark and open the quilt to check that any strong design elements such as stripes, are matching. Pin at those points to insure that they will match.

6. Re-fold quilt and begin sewing at the intersection point, and sew to edge of border, **Fig 14**; backstitch. Open the quilt and check the miter. Press the seam open, double check that the design matches and the corner is flat; trim the excess border to ¹/₄".

Fig 14

How to Mark Quilting Designs

Where to put quilting stitches depends on the pattern and set of the quilt. You can quilt "in the ditch" by following seam lines outlining the basic design elements or color changes. "By the piece" quilting can be stitched without marking by setting the needle just inside the ¹/₄" seam allowances. You can mark decorative designs over the plain or patchwork areas of the quilt.

Prepare the quilt top for marking by pressing the entire quilt top.

Always test the marker you plan to use for marking the quilting designs. Chalk markers that brush off can be used for simple grids and straight lines. Mark a block at a time, as the chalk does not handle well. White and silver pencils should be used with a light touch and should be kept sharp. Use a scrap of polyester batting to help rub off their marks. Water soluble markers require cold water on the quilt, so be sure you have pre-washed all the materials used.

How to Layer the Quilt Top, Batting and Backing

1. Measure the width and length of the quilt through the center. Cut and assemble the backing so that it extends two inches beyond the quilt top on all sides. Press seams open for ease in quilting.

2. Check the batting package. Some cotton-blend batts require prewashing, and some polyester batts should be tumbled in a dryer with a damp washcloth to relax the fold lines.

3. Place the backing, wrong side up, on a large table or clean carpet. Tape or pin to keep lining taut. Keep the corners square.

4. Spread batting over backing and trim batting to same size as backing.

5. Center quilt top on batting and backing. Starting at center of the quilt, pin all three layers together with 1" safety pins. Working out from the center, pin about every 8".

6. Loosen the tape, or edge pins. Fold the backing over the batting and pin to "seal" the edges. Begin quilting in the center of the quilt and continue from the center out. Work to make your stitches even, not just small.

How to Make Bias Binding

The following instructions for Continuous Bias Cut with Rotary Cutter are from Jackie Reis of Accu-Patterns.

Making the Continuous Bias Strip

1. When over one yard (in length) of bias edging is needed, use a calculator and the following method to determine the size of the fabric square required.

   a. Find the distance, in inches, around the quilt: two lengths plus two widths.

   b. Add 10 inches for mitering corners and overlap.

   c. Multiply this number by the width of the binding you plan to cut.

   d. Push the "square root" symbol on the calculator. Round to the next highest whole number and add the width of the binding you plan to cut.

Example: The quilt measures 102" x 104"

   a. 102 + 104 = 206 (length plus width)
      206 x 2 = 412 (distance around quilt)

   b. 412 + 10 = 422
      (perimeter plus allowance)

   c. 422 x 2 = 844"(length to cut binding)

   d. square root of 844 = 29.052 round to
      30 and add 2 = 32" square required.

2. Once you have the size of the square needed, cut it in half diagonally, **Fig 15**. Place pieces, right sides together, to form a "giant tooth"; offset the edges, then sew together by machine using a $^3/_8$" seam allowance, **Fig 16**. Press seam open.

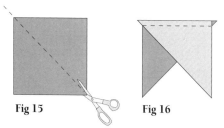

Fig 15   **Fig 16**

3. Place fabric on cutting board with wrong side of fabric touching the board and bias edges parallel to the length of the board, **Fig 17**.

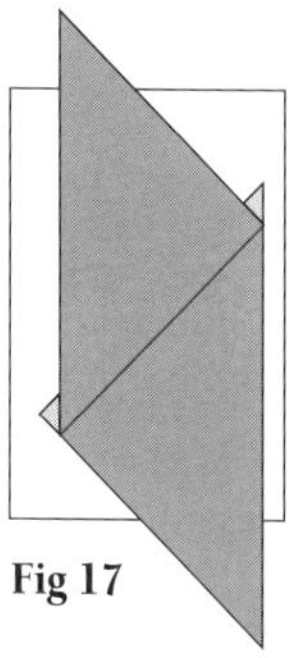

4. Fold upper tip of fabric down to seam line, **Fig 18**; fold lower tip up to seam line so the straight grain edges meet diagonally but do not overlap the butting line.

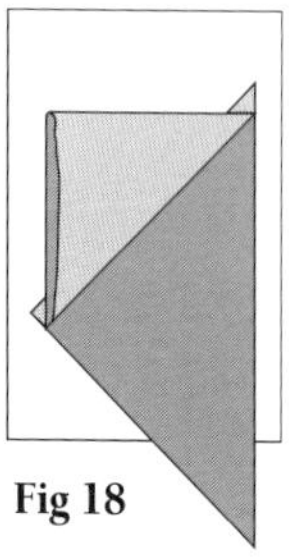

5. Keep bias edges even on left side and as even as possible on the right. (Left-handed users, re-verse these directions.)

Fig 17

Fig 18

Fabric will be two thicknesses. Begin cutting the width desired from the left (lefties on the right) using rotary cutter, mat, and acrylic ruler. The cut will "jump across" the butting line; that is, stop the cutting 1" before the line and start again 1" after the line. Continue to cut across the width of the fabric with parallel cuts, jumping across the butting line

on each cut. Cut through and discard the last incomplete row, **Fig 19**.

6. Referring to **Fig 20**, gently lift up the tip of the first row and use scissors to cut through to the end of fabric (See **A+**); gently lift up the tip of the last row and cut through to the end of fabric (see **B**).

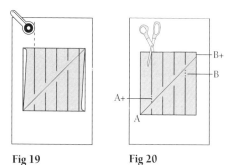

Fig 19   **Fig 20**

7. Gently slide and align the fabrics at the butting line so that **A** is even with **A+** and **B** is even with **B+**, **Fig 21**. With right sides together join butted edges together with a $^3/_8$" seam allowance forming a tube.

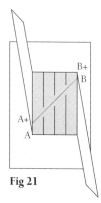

Fig 21

8. Slide the fabric tube over the ironing board; press seam open. Using a good pair of fabric scissors, cut across uncut portions of fabric making a long, continuous strip, **Fig 22**. Unwind bias strip from board.

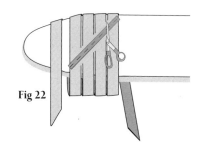

Fig 22

If you are making a doubled binding, press strip in half lengthwise with wrong sides together.

Sewing Binding to Quilt (for Mitered Corners)

1. Leaving a 6" to 8" tail, place binding right sides together with layered quilt (quilt top, batting and lining) along raw edge; sew binding to quilt, using a ¼" seam allowance, to within 8" from a corner. If necessary, adjust distance to avoid having a binding seam fall at the corner.

2. Continue to stitch binding to within ¼" of edge of quilt top, **Fig 23**. (If you are using a larger seam allowance, you will stop at that distance from edge.) Backstitch to anchor.

Fig 23

3. Fold binding to back of quilt and finger crease binding at fold, **Fig 24**. Bring the creased fold to the top of the quilt corner and begin stitching where previous stitching stopped, **Fig 25**; backstitch to anchor.

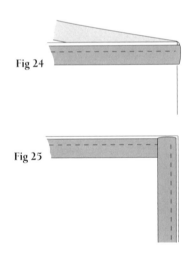

Fig 24

Fig 25

4. If you approach a corner and find that a seam will fall in the corner miter, cut off the binding diagonally two or three inches before the corner turn. Rejoin bias strip in a diagonal seam and continue sewing bias to quilt, turning remaining corners in same manner.

Final Joining of Binding in a Diagonal Seam

1. Stop stitching about 8" from beginning stitching. Tails should overlap several inches. Insert a straight pin into the quilt in the middle of the joining space, **Fig 26**.

Fig 26

2. Pin strips together, but not to quilt, at the point where the pin is in the quilt, **Fig 27**. Binding should fit "comfortably" along unsewn edge. Remove pin in quilt.

Fig 27

3. Measuring from the binding pin, cut the strips one half the width of the binding. (If binding is cut 2", each strip is cut 1" from the pin, **Fig 28**.)

Fig 28

4. Remove binding pin, open left strip wrong side up (**A**), open right strip right side up (**B**), **Fig 29**. Place end **A** at right angle to, and on top of end **B**, **Fig 30**; pin. Stitch diagonally across the joining to form a triangle, **Fig 31**; remove pin.

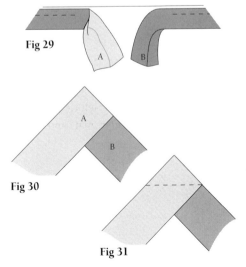

Fig 29

Fig 30

Fig 31

5. Open binding; refold on fold line if using a doubled binding. The distance of the unsewn binding should match the unsewn distance of the quilt. Trim off excess triangle of seam allowance, **Fig 32**; finger press seam open, stitch to quilt.

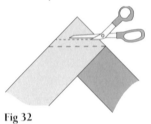

Fig 32

Finishing the Binding

Using thread to match binding, hand stitch binding to quilt back, covering the seam allowance.

At corners, use thumb nail to encourage miter on front of quilt. Fold binding over, then up on back of quilt, **Fig 33**. For the ultimate look, sew your miters closed on the front and back.

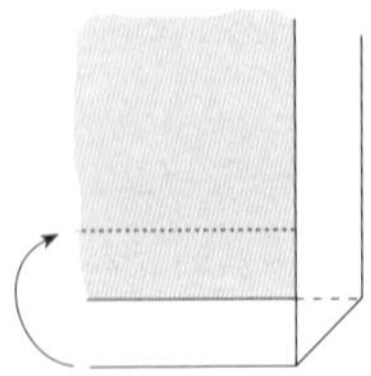

Fig 8

How to Sign and Date Your Quilt

Signing a quilt can be a simple matter of writing your name with a permanent fabric pen, or an elaborate cross stitch project, embellished with embroidery. Some quilt makers stitch their name and the date in the quilting design.

Include the name of the quilt maker (add your maiden name; it will soon be forgotten otherwise), the date the quilt was finished, and the city and state where the quilt maker lives. Use the label to tell the story of the quilt. What is the pattern? Was it made as a gift? Give as much information as possible.

Note: *Pigma® fine point pens don't bleed when used on fabric. Iron a square of muslin onto the shiny side of a piece of freezer paper to stabilize fabric for ease in writing. Practice writing slowly. Be sure to remove the paper before stitching the label onto the back of the quilt.*

Carpenter's Wheel

This quilt pattern has a long history and many other names including Star of Bethlehem, Sunflower, and Star Within a Star. Earlene Couch chose only brown print scraps in light, medium, and dark for piecing. She special cut the center diamonds from striped fabric.
Anne Brann completed the quilting in return for a quilt top pieced by Earlene.

Approximate Size 84" x 84"

Fabric Requirements:

4³⁄₄ yds of dark prints
1¹⁄₂ yds of light prints
4 yds of medium prints
2¹⁄₂ yds border print
1 yd dark print for binding
5³⁄₄ yds muslin backing
batting

Pattern Pieces (page 8):

A Diamond
B Square
C Border Triangle
D Border 1
E Border 2

Cutting Requirements:

Dark prints
400 A Diamonds
100 B Squares
Medium prints
400 A Diamonds
Light prints
520 B Squares
Border print
twenty C Border Triangles
sixteen D Border 1
eight E Border 2
four 2³⁄₄" x 86" strips

Sewing Instructions

Note: *Read Hand Piecing, page 2, before beginning.*

Shown in color on page 9.

Making the Star Block

1. Sew a lt print B Square to a dk print B Square, sewing ***along marked line only***, **Fig 1**. Sew lt print B Square to adjacent edge of dk print B Square, **Fig 2**. Repeat three more times.

2. Sew dk print A Diamond to lt print B Square, sewing on marked line, **Fig 3**. Sew another dk print A Diamond to adjacent edge of Square, **Fig 4**. Sew seam in Diamonds stitching from corner of square to edge of Diamonds, **Fig 5**. Repeat three more times.

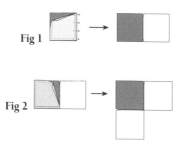

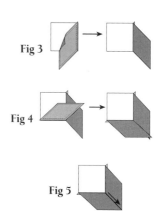

3. Sew med print A Diamonds to remaining sides of lt print B Square from step 2; sew seam in Diamonds from corner of Square to edge of Diamonds, **Fig 6**. Repeat three more times.

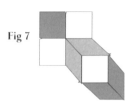

Fig 6

4. Sew units from step 1 to units from step 3, **Fig 7**; sew from inner corner toward outer edge.

Fig 7

5. Sew two dk print A Diamonds together creating half the center star, **Fig 8**; repeat.

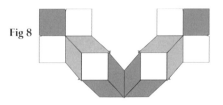

Fig 8

6. Join the half stars, **Fig 9**.

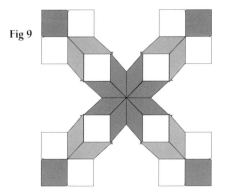

Fig 9

7. Sew two med print A Diamonds to a lt print B Square referring to step 2; join seam in Diamonds, **Fig 10**. Repeat three more times.

Fig 10

8. Sew a dk print A Diamond to each lt print A Diamond, for a "crown unit," **Fig 11**. Repeat for three more "crown" units.

Fig 11

9. Stitch "crown" unit into star, matching seams and sewing from inner corner toward outer edge, **Fig 12**.

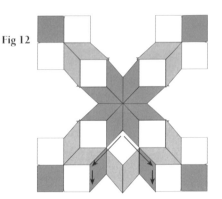

Fig 12

10. Repeat for three remaining sides to complete Star Block, **Fig 13**.

Fig 13

Star Block

11. Repeat steps 1 through 9 for a total of 25 blocks.

Joining the Blocks

1. Place blocks referring to layout. Sew two lt print Squares to one side of a Star block; sew two more Squares to adjacent side, **Fig 14**. Repeat for four more Star blocks.

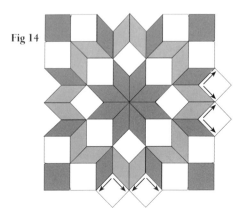

Fig 14

2. Sew five blocks together to complete a row, **Fig 15**. Repeat for four more rows.

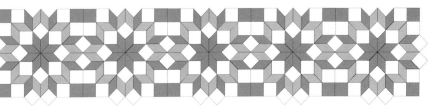

Fig 15

3. Sew rows together.

4. Sew lt print Squares in remaining spaces along two sides of quilt top.

Adding the Border

1. Sew Border Triangles, Short Borders, and Long Borders to fill in sides of quilt, **Fig 16**.

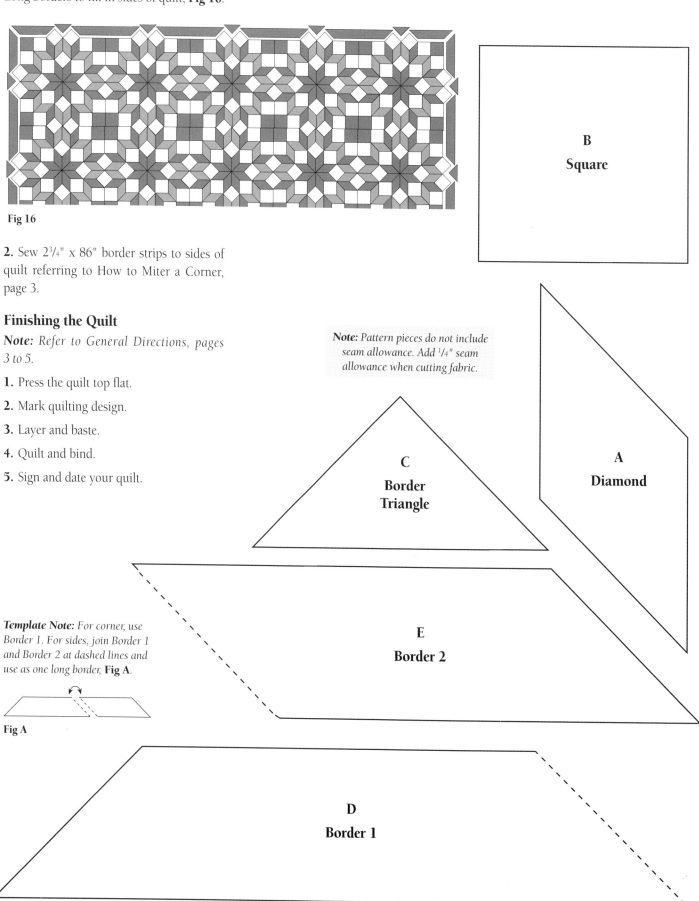

Fig 16

2. Sew $2^3/_4$" x 86" border strips to sides of quilt referring to How to Miter a Corner, page 3.

Finishing the Quilt

Note: Refer to General Directions, pages 3 to 5.

1. Press the quilt top flat.

2. Mark quilting design.

3. Layer and baste.

4. Quilt and bind.

5. Sign and date your quilt.

B
Square

Note: Pattern pieces do not include seam allowance. Add $^1/_4$" seam allowance when cutting fabric.

C
Border Triangle

A
Diamond

E
Border 2

Template Note: *For corner, use Border 1. For sides, join Border 1 and Border 2 at dashed lines and use as one long border, **Fig A**.*

Fig A

D
Border 1

8

Carpenter's Wheel, *page 6*

Chain of Diamonds, *page 13*

Stars & Flowers, *page 19*

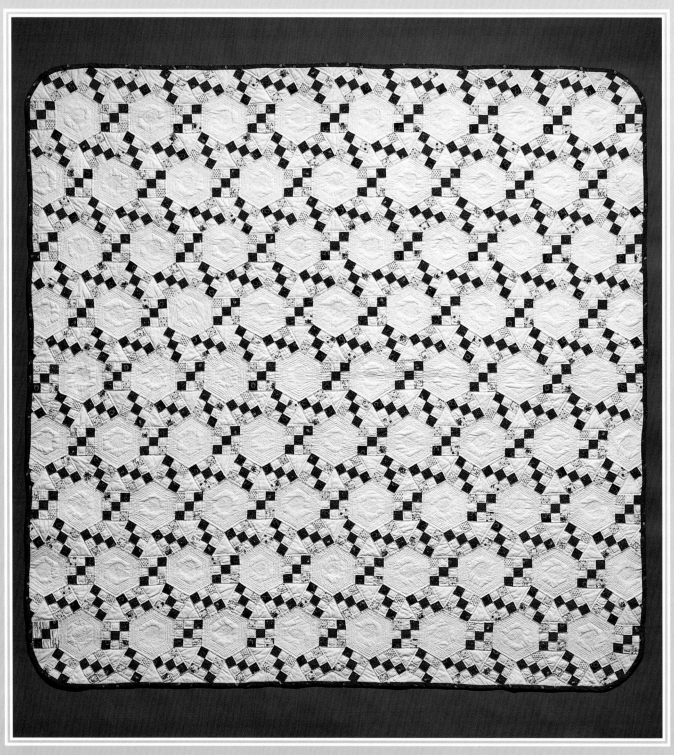

Jack's Chain, *page 16*

Chain of Diamonds

Earlene Couch is a prolific quilt maker. She sews many traditional patterns and adds her own touches such as appliquéd flowers in the corners of her Lone Star quilts. She loves to piece, and often barters for the quilting by piecing two tops, one for herself and one for the person who quilts it for her. Earlene collects plaid fabrics and found they make a wonderful scrap quilt in this old pattern.

Approximate Size:
80¹/₂" x 101¹/₂"

Fabric Requirements:

3 yds lt plaid scraps

3 yds dk plaid scraps

5¹/₄ yds muslin

7³/₄ yds backing

batting

Pattern Pieces (page 15):

A Diamond

B Quadrilateral

C Background

D Square

Cutting Requirements:

Plaid

124 D Squares, lt plaid for Nine Patches

155 D Squares, dk plaid for Nine Patches

128 B Quadrilaterals, plaid for Stars

128 A Diamonds, plaid for Stars

2"-wide strips totaling 380" length, assorted plaids for binding

Muslin

124 C Backgrounds

two 6" x 84" strips for top and bottom border

two 6" x 106" strip for side border

Sewing Instructions

Note: *Please read Hand Piecing, page 2, before beginning.*

Shown in color on front cover and page 10.

Making the Nine Patches

1. Sew a dk plaid D Square to opposite sides of a lt plaid D Square, **Fig 1**; repeat.

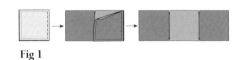

Fig 1

2. Sew a lt plaid D Square to opposite sides of a dk plaid D Square, **Fig 2**.

Fig 2

3. Sew rows to form Nine Patch, **Fig 3**.

Fig 3

4. Repeat steps 1 to 3 for a total of 31 Nine Patches.

Making the Star Block

1. Sew a plaid A Diamond to a plaid B Quadrilateral along drawn lines, **Fig 4**. Repeat three more times using the same plaid fabrics for each A and each B.

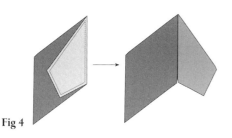

Fig 4

2. Sew two A/B units together along marked line forming half of a star, **Fig 5**; repeat.

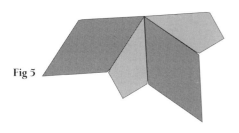

Fig 5

3. Join half stars to complete Star block, **Fig 6**.

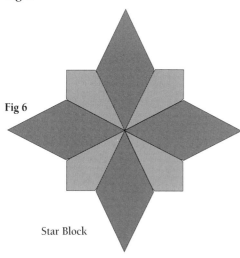

Fig 6

Star Block

4. Repeat steps 1 to 3 for a total of 32 Star blocks.

Joining the Blocks

1. Arrange Star blocks and Nine Patches as in layout on page 13.

2. Sew a muslin C Background to Nine Patch along marked line, **Fig 7**. Repeat along three remaining sides, **Fig 8**. Replace block in layout. Make 31.

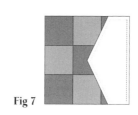

Fig 7

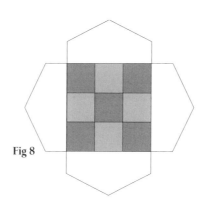

Fig 8

3. Sew Star blocks to adjacent edges of C Backgrounds along marked lines. Remember to stop and knot thread at the end of each marked line before going to adjacent edges.

Adding the Border

1. Center one side of quilt top on a 6" x 106" muslin strip; allow sufficient overlap for seam. Appliqué edge of quilt to border with a blindstitch, **Fig 9**, turning edge under as you sew. Repeat for opposite side.

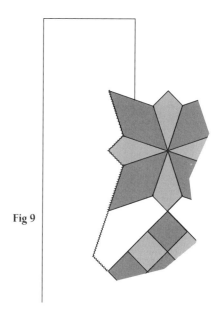

Fig 9

2. Repeat step 1 for top and bottom border strips.

3. Miter corners referring to How to Miter Corners, page 3.

Finishing the Quilt

Note: Read General Directions, pages 3 to 5.

1. Press entire quilt top.

2. Mark quilting design.

3. Layer and baste.

4. Quilt and bind.

5. Sign and date your quilt.

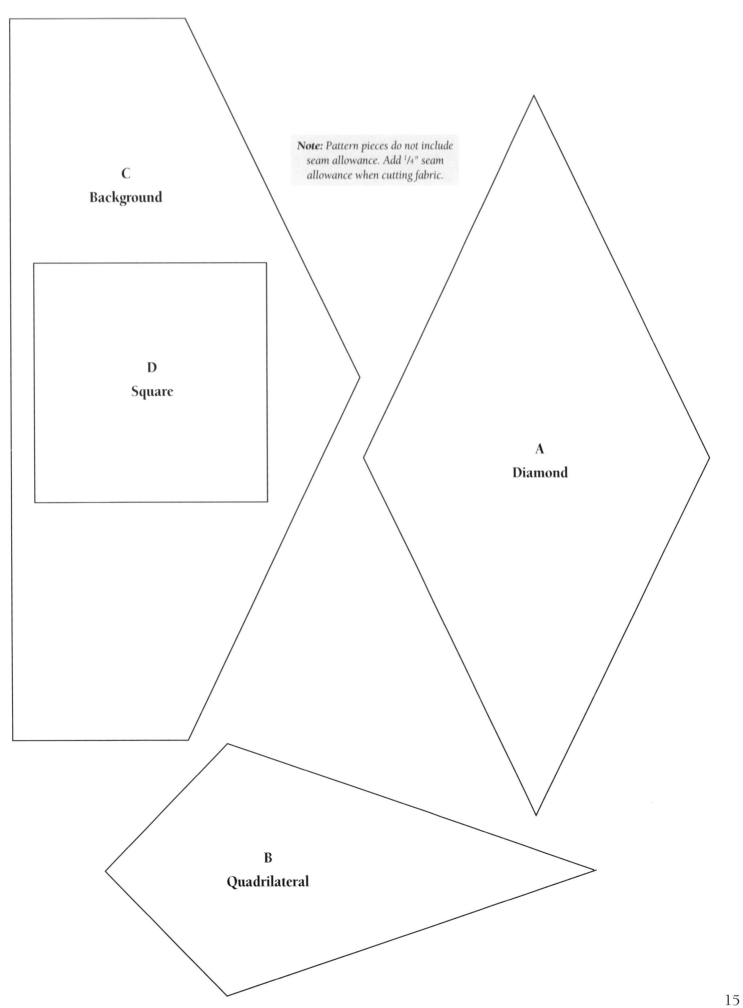

C
Background

D
Square

Note: *Pattern pieces do not include seam allowance. Add ¹/₄" seam allowance when cutting fabric.*

A
Diamond

B
Quadrilateral

Jack's Chain

Linda Jarvis wanted an easy pattern for her first quilt, so she chose the nine patch with a little different setting. Jack's Chain can be sewn in two colors or with many different colored scraps.

Approximate size: 79" x 79"

Fabric Requirements:

1⅝ yds red prints

¾ yd red on white prints

5 yds white

4¾ yds white for backing

¾ yd red for binding

batting

Pattern Pieces (page 18):

A Hexagon

B Triangle

C Triangle

D Square

Cutting Requirements:

White

980 D Squares

76 A Hexagons

170 B Triangles

14 C Triangles

Red prints

735 D Squares

Red on white prints

490 D Squares

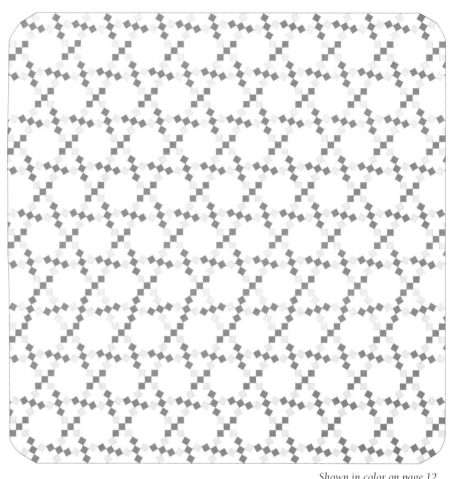

Shown in color on page 12.

Sewing Instructions

Note: *Read Hand Piecing, page 2, before beginning.*

Making the Nine Patch

1. Sew a red print D Square to white D Square along marked line, **Fig 1**. Sew a red/white print D Square to opposite side of Square, **Fig 2**. Repeat for another row.

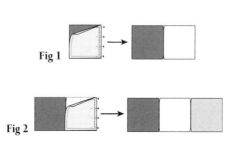

Fig 1

Fig 2

2. Sew a white D Square to opposite sides of a red print D Square, **Fig 3**.

Fig 3

3. Sew rows together to form Nine Patch, **Fig 4**.

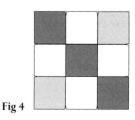

Fig 4

4. Repeat steps 1 to 3 for a total of 245 Nine Patches.

5. Cut eight Nine Patch blocks in half diagonally, **Fig 5**.

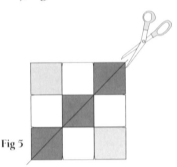

Fig 5

Joining the Blocks

1. Arrange A Hexagons, B and C Triangles, Nine Patches and half Nine Patches according to quilt layout. Sew together in rows as follows:

    a. eight Hexagons and nine Nine Patches, **Fig 6** (make five rows);

Fig 6

    b. nine Hexagons and eight Nine Patches, **Fig 7** (make four rows);

Fig 7

    c. sixteen Nine Patches, seventeen B Triangles and seven C Triangles, **Fig 8** (make two rows - one for top and one for bottom of quilt.);

Fig 8

    d. sixteen Nine Patches, seventeen B Triangles and two half Nine Patches, **Fig 9** (make eight rows).

Fig 9

2. Join rows to complete chains, stopping at the end of each drawn line and knotting thread before sewing adjacent edge.

3. Trim excess fabric from side edges, **Fig 10**.

Finishing the Quilt

Note: Read General directions, pages 3 to 5.

1. Press quilt top.

2. Mark quilting design.

3. Layer and baste.

4. Quilt and bind.

5. Sign and date your quilt.

Quilting Note: *Photographed quilt was quilted ¹/₄" inside edge of each Square, Triangle and Hexagon. There are five additional lines spaced ³/₈" apart with a heart quilted in center of each Hexagon.*

Fig 10

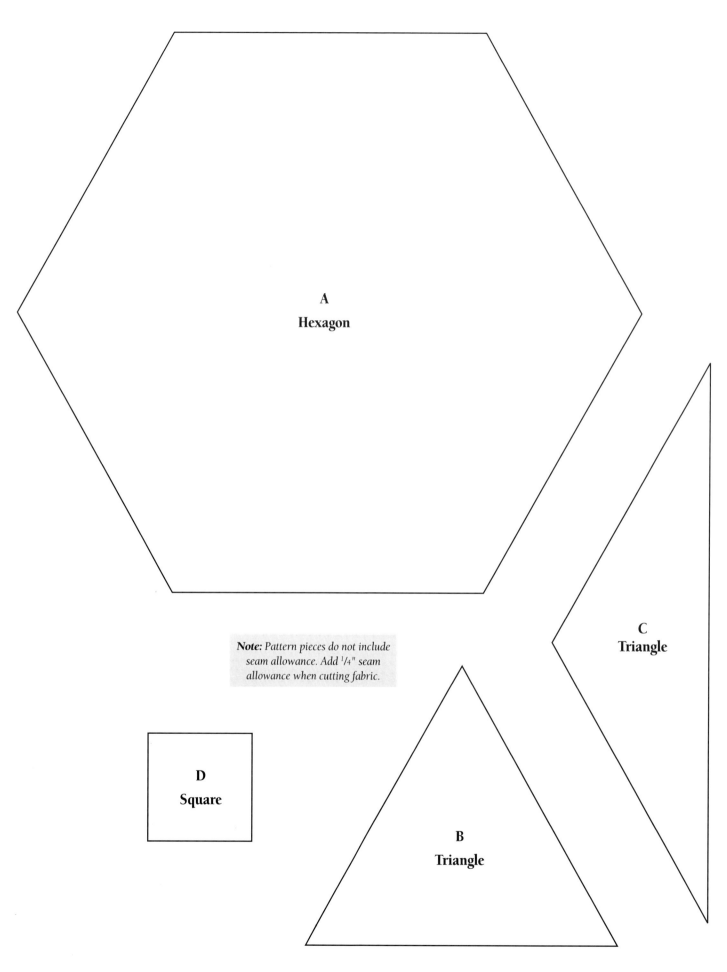

A
Hexagon

C
Triangle

Note: *Pattern pieces do not include seam allowance. Add ¹/₄" seam allowance when cutting fabric.*

D
Square

B
Triangle

Stars and Flowers

Sue McGann can do a trunk show of her scrap quilts and scrap quilt tops anytime the guild asks. Her talent for combining scraps produces unified multi-fabric traditional designs that demand closer study. This intricate pattern is sewn using only one pattern piece. The fabric choices provide a lesson in using the color values of the calicos.

Approximate Size: 96" x 90"

Fabric Requirements:

3¾ yds muslin center and edge
2¼ yds assorted dk prints
¾ yd assorted med/dk prints
1¼ yds assorted med prints
1¾ yds assorted lt prints
2¾ yds dk print for border
30" square for binding
2¾ yds 108"-wide muslin for backing
batting

Pattern Pieces (page 21):

A Quadrilateral
B Border Half Triangle

Cutting Requirements:

For each Star Block:
(Make ten)
30 A Quadrilaterals, muslin
18 A Quadrilaterals, dk print
twelve A Quadrilaterals, med dk print
twelve A Quadrilaterals, lt print

For each Flower Block:
(Make thirteen)
30 A Quadrilaterals, muslin
18 A Quadrilaterals, dk print
twelve A Quadrilaterals, med print
twelve A Quadrilaterals, lt print

For each Half Flower Block:
(Make four)
nine A Quadrilaterals, dk print
six A Quadrilaterals, med dk print
six A Quadrilaterals, lt print
fifteen A Quadrilaterals, muslin

Shown in color on page 11.

For Border (includes 2" extra length):
eight B Border Half Triangles
four B Half Border Triangles
two strips, 4" x 92"
two strips, 4" x 98"

Sewing Instructions

Note: *Read Hand Piecing, page 2, before beginning.*

Making the Star Blocks

1. Sew three muslin A Quadrilaterals together *along drawn lines only*, **Fig 1**; repeat.

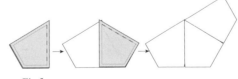

Fig 1

2. Join to form center hexagon, **Fig 2**.

3. Sew two dk print, two med print, and two lt print A Quadrilaterals to form a print hexagon, **Fig 3**. Make six.

4. Sew dark side of print hexagon on each side of center hexagon, **Fig 4**.

Fig 2

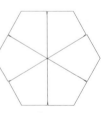

Fig 3

Fig 4

Shortcut for stitching hexagons: Stitch one print hexagon to center hexagon; don't knot off thread, **Fig 5**. Sew another print hexagon next to the first, stitching from the center out.

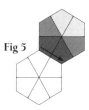

Fig 5

Baste back along the seam just sewn, then sew the second hexagon to the center hexagon, **Fig 6**. Sew each print hexagon to its neighbor before stitching to the center hexagon, **Fig 7**.

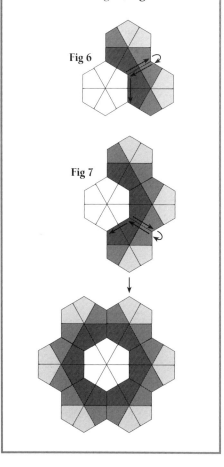

Fig 6

Fig 7

5. Sew a muslin A Quadrilateral to opposite sides of dk print A Quadrilateral forming the star points, **Fig 8**. Make six.

6. Sew two muslin A Quadrilaterals together, **Fig 9**. Make six.

Fig 8 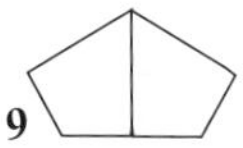   Fig 9

7. Sew star points and muslin units to hexagons to complete Star block, **Fig 10**. *Note: Follow shortcut and **Figs 4** through **6** to join pieces.*

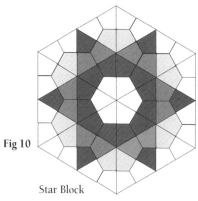

Fig 10

Star Block

8. Repeat steps 1 to 6 for a total of ten Star Blocks.

Making the Flower Blocks

Note: The Flower blocks are made the same way as the Star blocks. The placement of color gives the block its flower rather than star.

1. Sew six muslin A Quadrilaterals to form center hexagon, **Fig 11**.

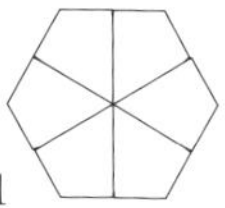

Fig 11

2. Sew two dk print, two med print, and two med dk print Quadrilaterals to form a print hexagon, **Fig 12**. Make six.

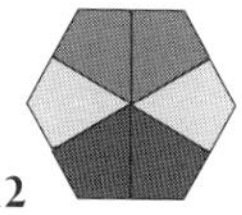

Fig 12

3. Stitch dark side of print hexagon on each side of muslin hexagon, noting position of hexagons, **Fig 13**.

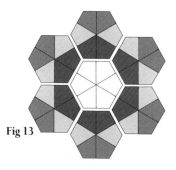

Fig 13

4. Sew two muslin Quadrilaterals to opposite sides of dk print Quadrilateral, **Fig 14**. Make six.

5. Sew two muslin Quadrilaterals together, **Fig 15**. Make six.

Fig 14   Fig 15

6. Sew all units together to complete Flower block, **Fig 16**.

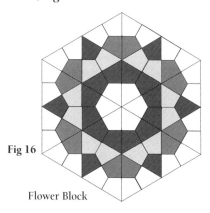

Fig 16

Flower Block

7. Repeat steps 1 to 6 for a total of thirteen Flower blocks.

Making the Half Flower Blocks

1. Sew three muslin A Quadrilaterals together for center, **Fig 17**.

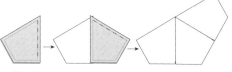

Fig 17

2. Sew two dk print, two med print, and two med dk print A Quadrilaterals together to form a print hexagon, **Fig 18**. Make two.

3. Sew one dk print, one med print, and one med dk print A Quadrilaterals forming a print half-hexagon, **Fig 19**. Make two.

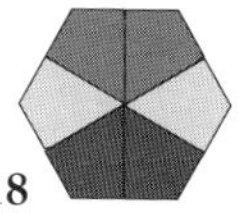

Fig 18    Fig 19